CHERRY MOON

LITTLE POEMS BIG IDEAS
MINDFUL OF NATURE

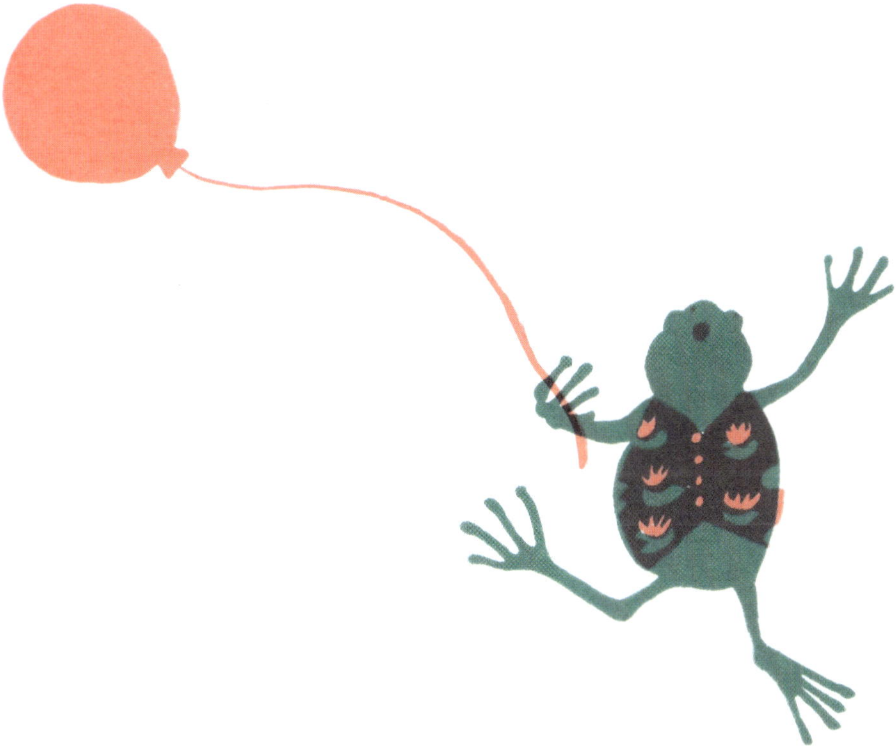

DEDICATION

Victoria, Gideon, Thatcher, Jacquelyn, Joseph, Fiona, Arlo and Gareth -Z.W.

Published in 2023 by Welbeck Editions
An Imprint of Welbeck Children's Limited,
part of Welbeck Publishing Group.
Based in London and Sydney.
www.welbeckpublishing.com

First published by ZaZaKids Books 2019

Text copyright © Zaro Weil 2019
Illustrations copyright © Junli Song 2019

Zaro Weil and Junli Song have asserted their moral rights to be identified as the author and illustrator of this Work in accordance with the Copyright Designs and Patents Act 1988.

All rights reserved. No part of this publication may be reproduced, stored in a retrieval system, or transmitted in any form or by any means, electronically, mechanical, photocopying, recording or otherwise, without the prior permission of the copyright owners and the publishers. A CIP catalogue record for this book is available from the British Library.

ISBN 978 1 80338 084 1

Designed by Sarah Pyke

Printed in China

10 9 8 7 6 5 4 3 2 1

CHERRY MOON

LITTLE POEMS BIG IDEAS
MINDFUL OF NATURE

Zaro Weil

illustrated by Junli Song

WELBECK
EDITIONS

morning

*I want to be
where wild things are
and be part of
well*

everything

ACKNOWLEDGMENTS

One day when I was little, I went for a walk with my father in the woods. It was May. Sunset. Looking up, the sky slid into pink wisps as the woods turned a strange, incandescent green. Some birds took off, shaking the leaves as they flew away. A squirrel raced up one of the trees. The full moon now looked almost red. Like a distant ripe cherry.

I took my father's hand because nothing had ever felt so perfect to me. So mysterious. Or powerful.

I never forgot that twilight in the woods; that pink and green sunset, the flying birds, the racing squirrel and that cherry moon.

These pictures stayed with me, as vivid as ever, until they conspired to persuade me to recreate that electrifying sense of oneness with nature I had experienced all those years ago. And that is how I came to write Cherry Moon.

Another inspiration was seeing the magical artwork of Junli Song for the first time.

And to readers out there who dare to dream big, think wild and long to experience nature in new and mysterious ways, it is for you I have written this book.

Contents

Listen earth	10
Snoring dog	12
Giddy with dawn	13
Plum tree (spring)	15
Snapping turtle's haiku	19
After the purple rains	20
How does the flower open	24
Tip-top of the world	26
Red red red	28
Dogwood flower	32
Pipsqueak	32
Strawberry	33
Bluebells	33
Such luck	35
Just-born bugs	36
Little jellybean toe shoes	36
Gosling's haiku	37
Hippo's haiku	37
River's haiku	38
River's song	39
Life is big	42
The linden tree is out	44
Wonderfulness	46
I spot them	48
Daytime	50
Be quiet sun	50
Shiny sun	50
Hum and buzz	51
A parade of beast-doodles	52
You and the stars	56
Moon things	56
Thorny branches	56
Worm's haiku	57
Cherry moon	59

Flicker and flash	60
Waterfall's song	64
Small green frog's song	66
Ladybird's song	67
This tiny bean	68
Dappling sun	72
Plum tree (summer)	74
Wild as the wind	78
Bats	81
Me without myself	82
Ten ways to catch the moon	84
Song of being together	87
Elephant tusks	88
When I heard the nightingale	93
Song of summer	94
Flash	96
Tell me a story	98
This great old tree	100
Between the cracks	104
How does the stone smell	105
Plum tree (autumn)	106
Wilderness howls	110
Tiny tiny bird	112
Mountain's song	114
Wind's song	114
Time's song	115
Every little pebble's song	115
Mixumgatherum	117
How to get lost	118
The leaves were a-shake	122
Don't be bored rock	124
This way and that	127
Mudpuddling tonight	128
When the beast	131

Fat moon	133
Hide and seek	134
Plum tree (winter)	137
Fairy lights	140
Silence	141
If all clouds were earth	142
Polar bear's haiku	145
Duskingtide	148
All tangled up	150
This day is too big	150
Thank you tree	151
Poor snail	153
Letter to the moon	154
Stop the world	156
Flea's haiku	158
Whale's haiku	158
Rain's haiku	159
Noisy toe's haiku	159
Story time orchestra	161
A confetti sky	162
Afternoon showers	162
Morning's haiku	163
Twilight's haiku	163
Perfect crystal's haiku	164
Snowy owl's haiku	164
Snow's song	165
Such luck again	166
Winter sun's haiku	167
Crunchandslide	169
Preposterous penguins	171
Trees and me	175
CLPE Notes	182
About the author and illustrator	192

LISTEN EARTH

listen earth

make sure
your buried rainbows
come up today
just like last spring

and a million springs
before that

SNORING DOG

can you hear that sound?
that's my dog snoring
he wakes up the stars
who wake up the moon
who wakes up the sea
who wakes up the earth
who wakes up the trees
who wake up the birds
who wake up

me!

GIDDY WITH DAWN

not even light and
the birds are
giddy with dawn
every one a-warbling from
slate-shadowed branches
every one a-winging through
just waking leaves
every one a-roistering under
a velveteen soft
up-rising sun

PLUM TREE (spring)

rollicking pink puffs
tremble under
woolly March clouds
wind's blowing hard

hang on blossoms

birds and I
grow ripe with worry

SNAPPING TURTLE'S HAIKU

snapping turtle

did you slow-step
all the way from the

dinosaur age?

AFTER THE PURPLE RAINS

after the purple rains

restless clouds of

crayon-box wildflowers

hurtle and tumble

skimble-skamble

harum-scarum

helter-skelter

in between rock beds

over squelchy slopes

through stone walls

to up-pop

outside my window

how very luck-dazzle

how very spring

HOW DOES THE FLOWER OPEN?

Q how does the flower open
A in petal time

Q how does the rain fall
A in drop time

Q how does the bird fly
A in wing time

Q how does the sea roll
A in wave time

Q how does the dog talk
A in bark time

Q how does the tree grow
A in root time

Q how does the cloud form
A in puff time

Q how do the planets travel
A in star time

Q how does the earth turn
A in all the time

TIP-TOP OF THE WORLD

such a quiet sky

can't hear you at all today
not even one note of blue
for this afternoon
fine fine water
floats down from the
tip-top of the world
soft-spreading a silent song
a thick grey cloud over
everything

such a quiet sky

with only
a festival of frogs
singing here
leaping there
catching the delicious mist
on their long tongues

RED RED RED

each year I'm waiting

for the cherries to ripen

each year I'm waiting

for the birds to eat them all

each year I'm waiting

to get there first

chirp chirp chirp

laugh the fat-bellied birds

merrily hopping over

last night's sticky sweet

red red red carpet of

beautifully pecked pits

DOGWOOD FLOWER

this dogwood flower and I met yesterday
we were both very pleased
and spent a long time
thanking one another
for summoning
such a scrumptious
sunny afternoon

PIPSQUEAK

. . . and have we discussed
the pipsqueak blossoms
on minuscule stems
buried in tiny
grass spears?

STRAWBERRY

if I were as red as you
as sweet
as round
I'd wind up in a basket too

BLUEBELLS

sprung from blue sky
fed by green rain
pushing always
towards April

and me

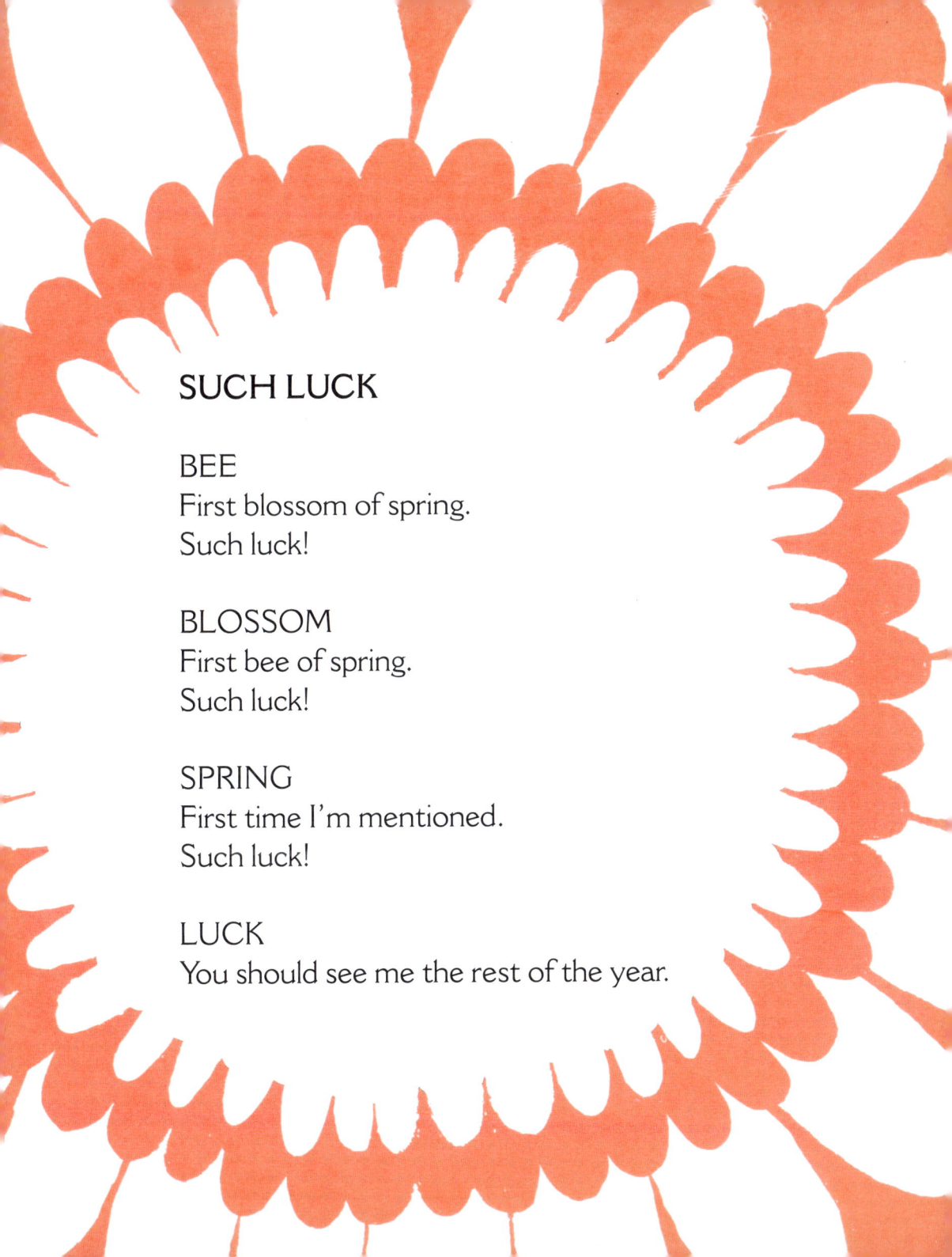

SUCH LUCK

BEE
First blossom of spring.
Such luck!

BLOSSOM
First bee of spring.
Such luck!

SPRING
First time I'm mentioned.
Such luck!

LUCK
You should see me the rest of the year.

JUST-BORN BUGS

wriggles of
tiny shadows in the dirty pond
inky live threads flitting by

look!

just-born bugs
and already
etching out their first spring

LITTLE JELLYBEAN TOE SHOES

this kitten wears
little jellybean toe shoes
underneath her paws
so when she jumps
she leaps
so high

so sweet

GOSLING'S HAIKU

good golly
giggled the gaggle
of googly-eyed goslings

seen mama?

HIPPO'S HAIKU

think slow
take my time
squish my toes
in muddy water

dig my fine shine

RIVER'S HAIKU

you'd never guess

                but it's taken forever

                                learning to roll

        so well

RIVER'S SONG

everyone
and I mean everyone
has something to say
to the river
some nod their heads and
take their time
others wave their arms or
race by talking
while some just listen

to what the river has to say

LIFE IS BIG

life is big
thought the grasshopper
landing in
green folds
between
grass blades

life is big
thought the snake
slithering fat coils
along the
rusty fence

life is big
thought the beetle
scuttling over the
rustling
aspen leaf

life is big
thought the caterpillar
squeezing inside a
fresh cabbage

life is big
thought the ant
carrying the
apple seed
to its
nest

life is big
thought the mouse
zigzagging between
sugar-scented
weeds

life is big
thought the cat
staring hard
at the blue sky of
diving birds

life is big
thought the dog
chasing round
trees loud with
scampering
squirrels

life is big
thought the fly
circling a
thousand and one
times
round my head

life is big
I thought
seeing the
whole wide world
while walking home
real slow

THE LINDEN TREE IS OUT

the linden tree is out!
the linden tree is out!
cry the hungry new flutterbugs
as they anxiously follow
sweetened trails
loop through
dew-speckled air
fly breathless in and out of a
tender-leafed canopy
all the way to a

single beckoning linden flower

they can finally call home

WONDERFULNESS

there it is

opening in a burst
of honeyed sundrops
right before my eyes

that rarest of rare plants
a bee orchid

looking just like a delicate yellow-black bee
sucking a fragile yellow-purple-black orchid

but instead of stopping
breathless to

admire its wonderfulness and
springfulness

I walk right on by

        my head still in a fuzzy
        winter-clumsy cloud of
        must-dos and don't-forgets

I SPOT THEM

I spot them
just outside the gate
fields of bright red poppies
flinging themselves carelessly
with every shift of wind song

towards light and morning

DAYTIME

sun slow-soars
towards morning
night cracks open
light seeds scatter

everywhere

BE QUIET SUN

be quiet sun

frog is having a daydream
naturally he dreams of night
and a million moon songs

SHINY SUN

shiny sun
so bright
so tiny
I could pick you up
and hold you
in my hand forever

I even heard
some people call you

buttercup

HUM AND BUZZ

when the world is so yellow
the air so full of
hum and buzz
I just close my eyes
and breathe in big
and then

one more time

A PARADE OF BEAST-DOODLES

when I opened up today
and unwrapped the morning
I found a present

a sky full of clouds
all puff-pomps and shine-streaks
bubble-whites and lace-feathers
a canopy of stipple-shapes

a parade of beast-doodles and
all I could do was
lie down
to skybig
to clouddream
and wonder
what I might unwrap

this afternoon

YOU AND THE STARS

mud puddle
mud puddle
it seems such a long way
between you and the stars
but sometimes
I just want to roll
in you both

MOON THINGS

water swells
each day it
chases the shoreline
till
sea things
moon things
call it back

THORNY BRANCHES

pale quince blossoms
on thorny branches
thin fingers reaching out
to grab March
by the scruff

WORM'S HAIKU

in and out of earth
magic worms
excavating
tiny roads
expressly
for April

CHERRY MOON

cherry moon
smooth
red
so perfectly shined
were you ever really

a blossom

FLICKER AND FLASH

so many dragonflies

translucent whirligigs
each a tailspin
of flicker and flash
under this
perfumed peach sky

a thousand
tinselly rainbows
glance off wings
a million
miniature wind-curls
dance round them all

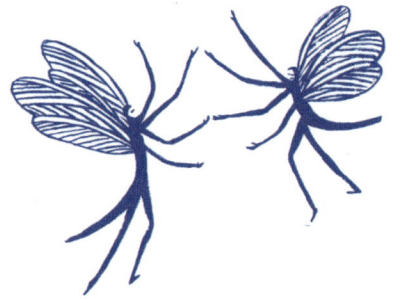

such capricious
summer sprites

cavorting forwards
hovering backwards

as though they have
all the time in the world
as though summer

will never end

WATERFALL'S SONG

born in some long-ago
    flicker of time
water arrives
    first
a fragile drop
a quiet trickle till
    another time-tremble
    sends it braiding through earth
surging all the way to
    today

        sheer-bubbling
        fast-flowing
        rock-rolling down cliffs
        a ceaseless torrent plunging
        into perpetual swirls
            dangerous dark pools

        and all the while
        crystalline spray wildly
            laces through air
        a bonanza of rainbow flecks
        sparkling with abandon

the wind is enchanted

hurriedly flies off
   (colourful new mist in tow)
vanishing in a breath from
today

only to be found
slow-seeping into
   long-ago legends
or trickling quietly

   into the future

SMALL GREEN FROG'S SONG

small green frog
hops onto the ridge
of the sticky jampot
of course
he's invited to tea

LADYBIRD'S SONG

yoohoo!
good morning!

have you seen
my new polka dots this season?
so perfect
each dot so
very very perfect!

what?

no?

OK
I'll tiptoe a little closer

wait!

don't be scared
I only eat
very very tiny things

THIS TINY BEAN

this tiny bean
was sprung from a bean flower
and fed by the sun
blue and yellow birds
sought it out
weightless butterflies
rested on its quivering petals
generations of insects
climbed up and down its
perfectly formed pod
rainbow water
splashed its roots

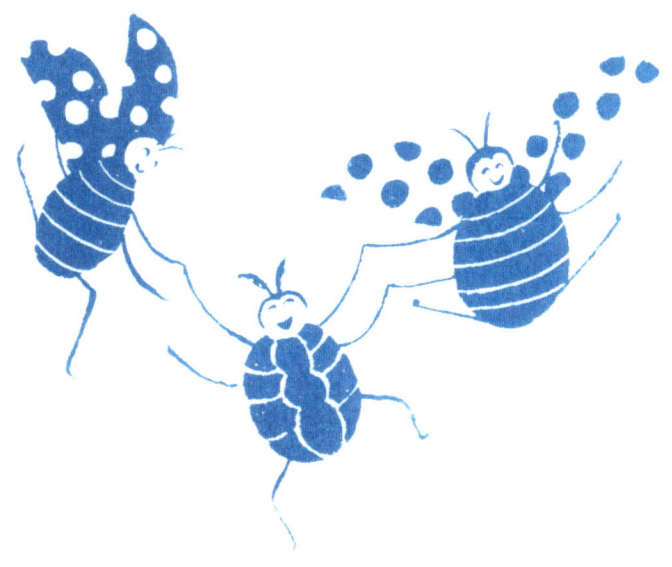

clearly
this tiny bean
was never in a million years
just any old
bean

DAPPLING SUN

dappling sun

                              bounces in dots

over petals and grass

                              jumps in sprinkles

from tree to tree

                              hops in flecks

all over the sidewalk

leaps in freckles

                round puddles and walls

so many speckles

                so many spots

so many skips

                so much summer

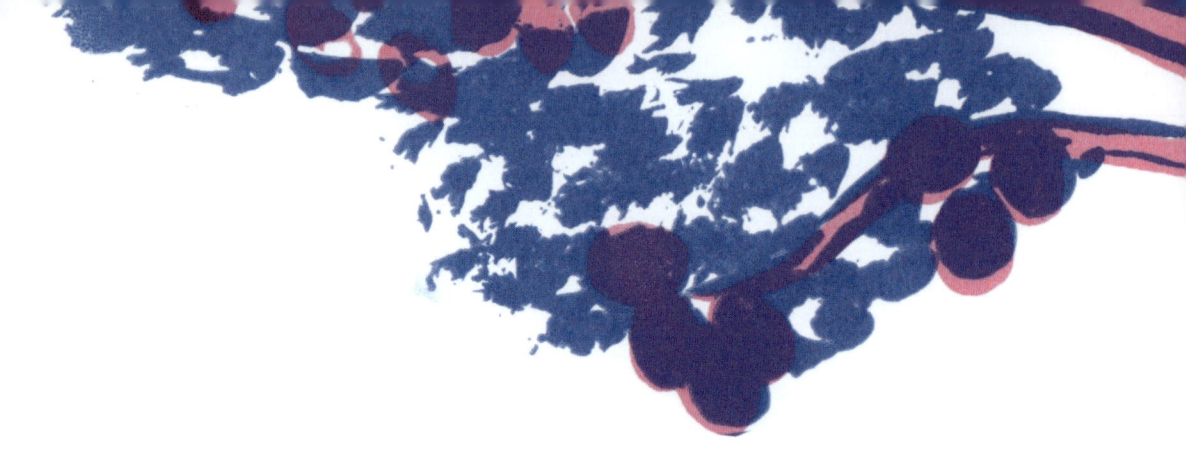

PLUM TREE (summer)

here at last
here at last
purple dripping like honey
down my chin

winter?
never heard of it

WILD AS THE WIND

if I were wild as the wind
I'd cannonball around the world

        atop a whizzing zigzaggery
        night-streaking through
        star spangles

    swaggering through sun whorls

        untameable
              unstoppable
                      uncatchable

if I were wild as the wind
I'd somersault all the way to
that dangerous terrible edge

    of far away
      where I'd gather my forces

          tempestuous
              tumultuous
                  turbulent

    and start again

BATS

almost midnight

bats dart
like phantom jets
round my head

really

can't they tell

I'm nothing like a bug

ME WITHOUT MYSELF

the sun has run away

spinning out of control
till in a sizzling flare of
electric yellow it
streaks towards earth
plunging headlong

right into my street

suddenly trapped   summer-hot colours
in the blinding glare   dissolve as
nothing dares move or   shadows peel off like
even breathe   cling film

                                        everything now laid
                                        flat
                                        white
                                        and no creature venturing out
                                        in search of cool or dark
                                        has a clue that they are
                                        missing a detail of themselves

their shadow

even my shadow
splits without a word
leaving me suspended

me without myself

so
I wait under a tree
like every other half-shape   for things shadowy to return
for twilight   cautiously
for the sun to come back   moon in tow
and tumble   rounding out the world till
like it always does   nothing is missing
behind the city

                                                  where we are all
                                                  reunited at last with those
                                                  moody tangles
                                                  deep folds
                                                  mythic twists

                                                  of darkness

TEN WAYS TO CATCH THE MOON

1 put it carefully into a jar of stars

2 paste it to your bedroom ceiling with strong shadows

3 wrap it with beams you borrowed from the sun earlier

4 save it in a special drawer next to your little silver comets

5 cast your fishing line very very far

6 climb a ladder to the top of everything

7 drop it in the water till it bounces over to you

8 ask the man who lives up there to throw it down to you

9 climb a tree and untangle it gently from the leaves

10 jump up and down till it loses balance and topples out of the sky

SONG OF BEING TOGETHER

when the river is together with its ripples
    it's one
when the grass is together with its green
      it's one
when the mountain is together with its peak
        it's one
when the moon is together with its shine
          it's one
when the tree is together with its leaves
            it's one
when the flower is together with its scent
              it's one
when the rain is together with its drops
                it's one
when the butterfly is together with its colours
                  it's one
when I sing and dance and make up stories
                    I'm one

ELEPHANT TUSKS

these long smooth tusks
are mine
passed down to me by
my family
who are older than your family
it would be very bad luck
for you humans
to take my tusks
you don't need them
besides
it is clearly my ancient
elephant right
to keep them

WHEN I HEARD THE NIGHTINGALE

when I heard the nightingale
it was so beautiful
I fastened my words
to the music

SONG OF SUMMER

giddily fat
slickly black
bugs
dazzled by sun-shimmer
fevered by heat-sting
rush on ungainly legs along scorched earth
squeezing themselves into some small
hollow of
some tree somewhere while
tiny hovering things
finding the sky too thin for flight
give up
head for a million dark spots
lilliputian places hidden beneath
in between and behind other places
to wait it out

till only the crickets
cunningly dotted on
branch leaf and stem
rub their legs together
as fast as they can in a
grinding
tuneless
completely reassuring

song of summer

FLASH

flash

just spotted the
brightest red
in the world the
glowingest orange
in the universe the
hottest blue
in the cosmos
all
on one
small bird
it was so bright
I had to look away

but the bird just smiled

and took off

in a flutter of razz-dazzle
soaring towards some new
tangerine-twizzle
of a galaxy

TELL ME A STORY

tell me a story
tell me now or
I will wait here
till earth sea moon and stars
all talk

all at once

THIS GREAT OLD TREE

this great old tree dreams
with its tangling hungry roots
daily pushing their way through
billion-year earth to
ancient buried water

this great old tree dreams
with its voluminous trunk
daily rounding and circling
slow ring by slow ring
growing century by century

this great old tree dreams
with its twisting branches
thrusting here turning there
daily seeking strands of
quicksilver light

this great old tree dreams
with its fragile veined leaves
trembling to every fresh
wind wave
daily searching sequinned
sky drops of water

this great old tree dreams
with its rope-knotted bark
daily giving shelter
to a universe of small creatures
who call it home

this great old tree dreams
with its boughs of fruit which
daily fall into the mouths of
beasts and birds
who grow fat from
such sweet food

this great old tree dreams
with its infinite summer shade
when I stop to
daily rest under its dappled arbour
to dream all the dreams
I can possibly dream

BETWEEN THE CRACKS

last night hides
between the cracks
starry night rolls in
under the door
yesterday's pale moon stretches
through my bedroom window
a galaxy of dust whirls
around my pillow
sunrise shadows
rustle the quiet

I wonder what's going to slip in next
through the very same cracks

HOW DOES THE STONE SMELL

how does the stone smell
how does the grass sound
how does the tree fly

however I say

how does the day roll
how does the moon spin
how does the cloud sing

however they feel

how does the cricket read
how does the lion think
how does the walrus talk

the way they always have

PLUM TREE (autumn)

plums
hope you're inside that branch
can't see a thing
but if I run up close
and open my ears

sap roars
like tree lions

WILDERNESS HOWLS

wilderness howls

when wind
carries the scent of
wildflower blaze

when trails of birds
thread gaudy air ribbons
between tree tangle

when water up-bubbles
to varnish earth in clear gleam
(rainbows where you'd least expect them)

when silky-shined rocks reveal lost paths
going dangerous spiky directions

when candy-coloured bugs feast inside
tiny leaf glints of sun shadow

it's all true
the world re-enchants

when wilderness howls

TINY TINY BIRD

sundown

tiny tiny bird
perches on top of the pine cone
watches my fading shadow
follows its every move and when
she flies off into sky blush
through a shake and shimmy of
dusk green needles
my shadow and I miss her
long to catch up

think it would be fun to
shake and shimmy our way as well
all the deep night
all the deep way to

sun-up

MOUNTAIN'S SONG

even if you can't see
over my peak
don't worry
I'll tell you a story later
about the other side

WIND'S SONG

so why wait?
come on
keep up
I'll get behind you

hey!
just helping

TIME'S SONG

on and
on and
on and
on
not ahead
not behind
stopping only for a
dream or two

EVERY LITTLE
PEBBLE'S SONG

I celebrate ancient earth
I salute ancient wind
I congratulate ancient waters

they made me who I am today

MIXUMGATHERUM

mixumgatherum
said the wise-talking wind
to the seed
then rainumandgrowum
and infivehundredyearsum
a mighty great
forest you'llbeum

HOW TO GET LOST

ask your shoes to walk you over the edge of the map
        or
fly off with your biggest fattest birthday balloon
        or
dive into the notes of your favourite song
        or
explore a hidden cave of stirring stories
        or
hitch a ride on anything exploring anywhere
        or
run your fingers over the globe till they can't remember where they started

       or
trade places with a time traveller
       or
dress up as a falling leaf and see where you land
       or
join an ant colony and journey to underground kingdoms
       or
hold on tight to the north wind
       or
travel quietly into the deepest forest you can find . . .
       or
            or
                 or
                      or
                           or . . .

THE LEAVES WERE A-SHAKE

the leaves were a-shake
they had heard the news
birds passed it on
moss spread the word
faded sunflowers told everyone
ivy twined it round
ducks splashed it out loud
spiders spun the story
ants mentioned it over and over
in passing
for everyone knew
tomorrow
autumn would be heading their way

naturally
the leaves got the picture and
overnight curled
yellowed and oranged
next
they signalled a crinkly wind-call
to each other
whispering in a thousand
thin rustles

time to take off
time to take off

DON'T BE BORED ROCK

don't be bored rock
once you were orange fire
thundering down some
mountain slope or
hurtling silver sleek
through deep sky

maybe you were thrown up
sputtering red by
an ancient fuming volcano or
born with the planet in a
starless galactic bang

to be carved sharp by ice
rounded by raging wind

but whichever it was
being still now is good
after all

you have so much to remember

THIS WAY AND THAT

the hills roll this way and that
covered in trees swaying this way and that
filled with leaves swirling this way and that
surrounded by birds flying this way and that
all adrift in the wind soaring this way and that
everyone knowing winter won't wait

MUDPUDDLING TONIGHT

mudpuddling tonight
sloshgurgling
all the way home through
a well-shined slipstream of
a million and one raindrops
lit by
a million and one moondots

WHEN THE BEAST

when the beast
swaggers and stomps
round my bed at night
it doesn't bother me
lemon drop stars
and a mango moon
are just outside

HIDE AND SEEK

I decided to play a game with quiet

hide and seek
my turn
I slipped into the woods
looking for quiet
instead
a cacophony of forest-crackle
a hullabaloo of beast-babble
sprang towards me while
a tweedledum of pandemonium
circled above
it was a free-for-all
and even the sun
jangled copper
between the leaves

so much for the forest

I went to the sea
searching for quiet
but the waves trumpeted
a rumbling ruckus
a crash of crinkle-crests while

squarking gulls sky-dived into
wind-trembled sea and
seashells crunched underfoot
as a medley of
fat green seaweed
slapped the sand
non-stop non-stop

so much for the sea

but then I turned
and quiet tagged me
I stopped
forest stopped
sea stopped

I found quiet
it must have been hiding
the whole time
inside my words
inside of me

PLUM TREE (winter)

you may not look like much now
however
if I stand under your branches
and wait a little while
juicy things will fall into my mouth
like sweet snow

FAIRY LIGHTS

fairy lights
after the storm
gossamer cloud drops
quiver under still
damp stars

SILENCE

silence waits
inside and out
and like my poem
takes its time

I have to be ready
to hear it

IF ALL CLOUDS WERE EARTH

if all clouds were earth
and all earth were skies
and all skies were suns
and all suns were stars
and all stars were rivers
and all rivers were rocks
and all rocks were fish
and all fish were mountains
and all mountains were birds
and all birds were trees
and all trees were people
and all people were flowers
then if I picked one flower

I'd hold absolutely everything
in my hand

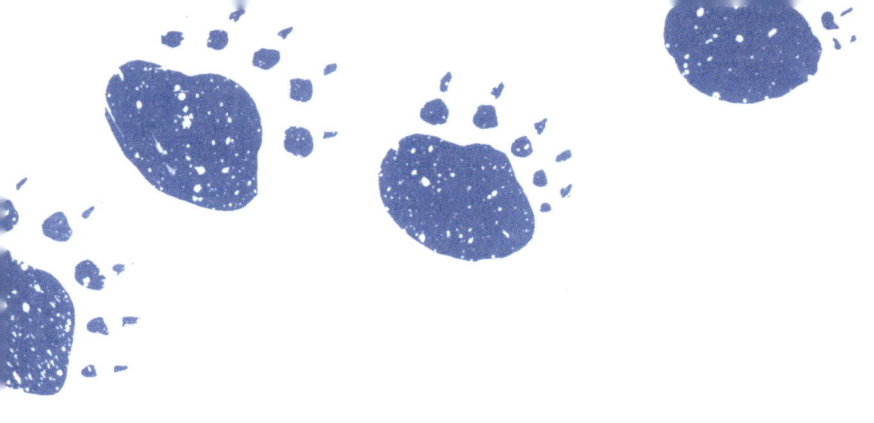

POLAR BEAR'S HAIKU

belly blank as snow
ache walks with each step
as hope melts
and fear drips
like ice

DUSKINGTIDE

somewhere
between
   the last second of day
   first second of night
between
   the daily swap
   of sun and moon

that shadowy veil between
light and dark vanishes in

a wizardly puff

the world is now bewitched
spellbound inside and out

forests are frosted in silver-leafed sleep

fiery red clouds harden into
   black-browed mountains
   clamorous sky creatures

a thousand lost spirits
are set loose in spectral air swirls

bouquets of buried stars
out-pop through purple sky-fields

telltale scents
twine round the low-flying moon

twilight's small sounds
amplify into a chorus of giants

till the deep loud duskingtide
this ancient gloaming
this breathless semi-dark
spins
in one incandescence
into pure night

and with just a
tiny candle-strike

is gone

ALL TANGLED UP

sorry
can't come right now
I'm all tangled up with these words
they're jumping east and
twisting west
itching to be untangled
into a poem

THIS DAY IS TOO BIG

this day is too big
this sky is too grey
this cloud is too fat
my shadow so small

POOR SNAIL

poor snail
crushed
by some careless foot

what other small
deaths

I wonder

lie hidden in
my garden

LETTER TO THE MOON

dear moon,
once you were so small
so barely breathing
that even the tiniest planets
laughed and danced circles
right over you each evening
and the silver studded comets
ignoring you completely
hurtled past all slapdash glee
towards nowhere special
plus your old friend sun
didn't bother to say a word before
merrily sailing off in some
great blood orange ball

but moon
I have always been here
waiting
every night
so I hope you sleep well
up there

your friend,
me

STOP THE WORLD

stop the world
so I can leap onto
a rainbow and
cartwheel down a
carnival of colour

stop the world
so I can watch
a galaxy of buds as
they unfurl into
starry flowers
slow blink by
slow blink

stop the world
so I can burrow inside
this jagged rock and
explore every ancient and
faraway place
it's ever travelled

stop the world
so I can caper with
the clouds and
float puff-like into
anything I want

stop the world
so I can run roaring
with the lions and
be on their team
whenever they need me

stop the world
so I can smell each
throbbing scent as it
circles and
whirls its way into
the big fat air

stop the world
so I can pop inside
a polka dot
and decorate any
bustling butterfly

stop the world
so I can plunge
under the sea and
discover every
fish-slippery
secret

stop the world
so I can rocket
through the stars
and count all the
zillions of light beams

stop the world
so I can scrunch up in a
soft-sailing snowflake and
see winter through
a prism of shiny crystals

stop the world
so I can look
inside myself and
discover all the

deep-down

ready-to-burst

hidden

magic

FLEA'S HAIKU

great jump!

awesome leap!

but if I really try . . .

zoom!

right over the moon!

WHALE'S HAIKU

born all the way in
lost long ago
I deep-dive to . . .

you'll never know

RAIN'S HAIKU

oh

the joy of falling

how exhilarating

becoming a

splash

NOISY TOE'S HAIKU

if I wiggle one toe
others join in
can't stop laughing
noisy toes

STORY TIME ORCHESTRA

a story time orchestra
lives inside my book
and when I open
to my favourite part

everyone starts to play

A CONFETTI SKY

when the sun
is finished
each day
it shreds into
a confetti sky
each night

AFTERNOON SHOWERS

colours grow loud
earth grows mud
scents grow long trails
all the way to sunset

MORNING'S HAIKU

morning rolls gentle
into good day
refolds the dark

untwines its light

TWILIGHT'S HAIKU

twilight blur

one by one
stars ignite
as night sky unveils

a slow bloom
moon

PERFECT CRYSTALS HAIKU

everywhere
newborn white flakes
perfect crystals
then gone
perfect riddle

SNOWY OWL'S HAIKU

oh
I sky roll a thousand paths
today

poor earth
can't turn very fast

SNOW'S SONG

I know
I know

hard to be quiet when I arrive
but look
outside is loud with
white puffs
and

not one little sound

SUCH LUCK AGAIN

SNOW
First icy wind of winter.
Such luck!

ICY WIND
First snow of winter.
Such luck!

WINTER
First time I'm appreciated.
Such luck!

LUCK
Told you . . . I'm totally great all year.

WINTER SUN'S HAIKU

guess who!

ice twinkles
snow sparkles
frost gleams

surprised?

it's me!
winter sun

CRUNCHANDSLIDE

when snow falls
everyone rushes to
standinaweandlook
when snow rests
everyone rushes
everywhichway to
crunchandslide then
crunchandslide
againandagainandagainand . . .

PREPOSTEROUS PENGUINS

thousands
of preposterously pensive penguins
pause to participate
in a particularly polar poetry pageant
probably in the perfectly pale and cold
penetrating South Pole
perhaps the precise problem is
every penguin parades around like
a posh peppy peacock
pretentiously presuming
to proclaim in a pesky pernickety way
they should (for pete's sake)
positively peep first

TREES AND ME

when night is still day
day still night
I head to the woods
to talk to the trees
I tell them bits and pieces
of this and that
they tell me of last winter
speak of new leaves
and whisper who passes
amongst their roots

and
when we're done talking
we sit quiet together
trees and me…

watching the sky
breathing the air until
we smile together
trees and me…

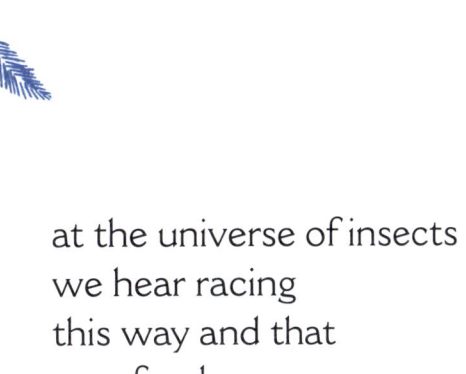

at the universe of insects
we hear racing
this way and that
way far down
under our feet
amongst our roots

trees and me…

twilight

*go gently
and let your eye be caught
by little things*

Exploring some of the poems in more depth

This book is a perfect invitation for adults and children to talk about and engage in the natural world, language and poetry together. Here are some ideas for how to explore some of the poems together in fun and engaging ways, provided by the Centre for Literacy in Primary Education; an independent charity that works with primary schools around the UK and beyond to support them in developing best practice in all aspects of literacy teaching.

CENTRE FOR **LITERACY** IN PRIMARY EDUCATION

LIFE IS BIG (PAGE 42)

Read and talk about the poem
Read the poem out loud together and discuss your initial impressions. *What did it make you think about? How did it make you feel? What made you feel this way?* Consider the title, *Life is Big*. *What does this mean to you? What do you think it means to the creatures in the poem?* Now, re-read the poem, considering the creatures described in each verse. *Who do you think the 'I' might be in the final verse? What language in the descriptions helps you to picture the creatures and their actions? How do you think each creature might be feeling in their verse? What in the words makes you think this? Is the caterpillar satisfied whilst squeezing into the cabbage? Is the mouse worried as it zigzags between the weeds? Do you have a favourite verse? Why is this?* Come back again to the title, *Life is Big*. *Do you ever have this thought? Why might life seem big at times? What might you do if this thought became overwhelming?* Consider how the poem focusses back on the little things in life; *what are the small things that you appreciate day to day?*

Explore the concepts
Think again about these creatures. *If you were going to order them from smallest to largest, which order would they go in?* Pick one of the verses, re-read it and think about the language that has been used to describe what the creature is doing. Take some paper and art materials and create an illustration of the verse. *How will you share the size and scale of the creature, in relation to the wider world around them to emphasise the title of the poem Life is Big?*

Perform the poem

Read the poem again, thinking about the actions of the creatures in the poem. *How could you perform the poem to emphasise these?* This could be through physical actions, but could also be the way in which you use your voice to emphasise the movements. *Will you pace lines or verses differently? Will some be faster or slower than others? Will you change the pitch or volume of your voice?* Consider the repetition of the line 'life is big'. *How will you say this at the start of each verse? Will you say it in the same way each time, or differently?* Consider how to use your facial expressions and body movements to add to the storytelling, making sure these add too, but don't detract from the meaning of the words and the emotions evoked by the poem. You could record yourself performing and watch this back to consider the effect you have created and the impact of your performance as you watch.

Activate your imagination

Consider other creatures that may have the same thought that *life is big*, who are not mentioned in the poem. Pick a creature and see if you can add your own verse to the poem about this creature. Think back to the original poem and the imagery created in the words that described the actions of the creature. Close your eyes and visualise your chosen creature. *What are they doing while thinking that life is big?* It may help to draw a sketch of your creature. This might enable you to think of language to describe this in your own verse. You might think of verbs to describe their actions, like *slithering*, *scuttling*, *squeezing*, *carrying*, in the original poem. You might think of how to add description using prepositions or adjectives, such as in the phrases *along the rusty fence*, *inside a fresh cabbage* or *between sugar-scented weeds*. When you've drafted your verse, think about how you will set it out on the page. *Where will you break the lines? Will you illustrate your verse?* Share your writing with a friend or family member.

THIS TINY BEAN (PAGE 68)

Read and talk about the poem
Read the poem out loud together and discuss your initial impressions. *What did it make you think about? How did it make you feel? What were you picturing in your mind as you heard the words? What words painted these pictures for you?* Re-read the poem for a second time. *How do you feel about the bean? What has the poet done to make you feel that way?* Consider the final line: *clearly this tiny bean was never in a million years just any old bean*. *What words or phrases make you think the bean is special? Why was this? How would you describe this bean, in a word, a phrase or a sentence?*

Explore the concepts
Find a seed, stone or bean that you can plant or grow. This could be a seed from inside a fruit you've eaten, like an apple, orange, pepper or chilli, a seed from inside a plum, nectarine or peach stone or a seed or bean that you have bought in a packet. Before you plant it, observe the seed carefully. *What does it look like? What is the shape and size of the seed? What colour is it? How would you describe it to someone else?* Think about what might happen when you plant it. *What do you think will happen? What might the plant look like when it grows? What will you need to do to help it to grow healthily?* Take time to observe and care for your seed as it grows, ensuring it has ample amounts of light, water and that the pot it is planted in has enough room for the growing roots. Keep an observation diary, tracking its growth. *How does what you see compare to what you thought would happen when you planted the seed?*

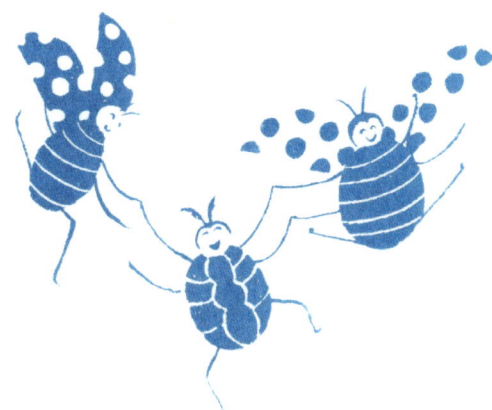

Perform the poem

Now, think about how what you have noticed could impact on a performance of this poem. *What will you bring to the performance that helps to show how the poet feels about the bean and the process of its growth? How could you use your voice? Should you dramatise any aspects of the performance? How will this add to and not distract from the meaning and feeling behind the poem?* Practice reading the poem through a few times, trying out different ideas and then invite a friend or family member to listen to you perform it. *Did they get a sense of wonder about the bean from your performance?*

Activate your imagination

Find a plant that is growing somewhere indoors or outdoors. It could be anything from a dandelion growing between the cracks in the pavement or a large potted plant in your home. Take some time to observe the plant closely. You might even draw it to help you really take in the plant in detail. *What is special about this plant for you? How could you describe it to someone else?* Think about the power of the words in the original poem and how magical the bean is made to sound through the words chosen to describe it. Use this to inspire your own poem about the plant you've chosen. You could illustrate your poem with a drawing of your plant.

ELEPHANT TUSKS (PAGE 88)

Read and talk about the poem
Read the poem out loud together and talk about it. *What do you think it is about? How does it make you feel? What makes you feel this way?* Re-read the poem again and focus carefully on the language. Consider the repetition of the words *me* and *mine* and *you* and *your*. *Who do you think is speaking in this poem? Who do you think they might be speaking to, and why? What do you think the line, it would be very bad luck for you humans to take my tusks might mean? Do you think this is a threat?* Now look at the illustration that accompanies the poem. *Why do you think the illustrator might have chosen to dress the elephant in human clothing, and have it standing on two legs?*

Explore the concepts
Read the poem again. *Why do you think a human might take an elephant's tusks? Why do you think the poet has chosen to highlight this in a poem? Do you know of any other animals who are endangered by humans? Why do you think this is?* If you have access to a smartphone, tablet, laptop or computer, access the WWF endangered species list: www.worldwildlife.org/species/directory. Look at how the list is categorised into *least concern*, *near threatened*, *vulnerable* (like the elephant), *endangered* and *critically endangered*. *What do you think these words mean? How do these words make you feel about the animals?* Pick an animal that you think people may want to support because of its extinction status. Look at the section headers, *Facts*, *Why they matter*, *Threats* and *What WWF is doing*. Make a note of information that you think might be useful in presenting the plight of the animal and to persuade someone that this is important and to help.

Perform the poem

Re-read the poem again. Discuss the feelings that the poem evokes in you. *How does it make you feel as you read? How do you think the elephant feels as it is saying these words? How does this compare with other poems, like Life is Big and This Tiny Bean? Do you think you would perform it in the same way as those poems? How might it be different? Do you think this is a loud poem or a quiet poem; or does it vary? What makes you think this?* Re-read the poem and think about how you might use your voice, facial expressions and body language to create the feelings you felt while reading and that the elephant might feel whilst saying the words. Practice a few times to perfect this. Consider how to use your facial expressions and body movements to add to the storytelling, making sure these add to, but don't detract from the meaning of the words and the emotions evoked by the poem. You could record yourself performing and watch this back to consider the effect you have created and the impact of your performance as you watch.

Activate your imagination

Create and shape a poem of your own about an endangered animal, using what you found effective in the original poem to inspire your own ideas or choices. You may wish to choose to write in role as the animal, addressing a human reader directly. Think about how you will celebrate your features, that are so highly prized by the human hunters and how you will show the anger and resentment towards what the humans are doing to put you in danger through your choice of words.

DON'T BE BORED ROCK (PAGE 124)

Read and talk about the poem

Read the poem out loud together and talk about it. *What do you think it is about? How does it make you feel? What makes you feel this way?* Re-read the poem and think about what happened. *What do you know about the rock? How long has it been around for? What journey has it taken, before it has reached this place? What happened to it on its journey? What does this make us think about the rock?* Now look back at the poem again, and think about the words and phrases that make the story of the humble rock sound powerful and dramatic. Think about the choice of adjectives in phrases like *orange fire, an ancient fuming volcano, raging wind*. What do these words add to our feelings about the rock and its importance in the world?

Explore the concepts

Use an encyclopedia or reference book to find out more about how rocks are formed. If you have access to the internet, you could use this page on the Britannica Kids website: https://kids.britannica.com/kids/article/rock/404136. *Why do you think the poet might have chosen a rock as the subject of her poem? What might be interesting or fascinating about rocks for her? What links can you see between what you read and what the poet has chosen to include in the poem?* Go outside and find a rock or pebble of your own. Hold it in your hand and think about how it might have been formed, based on what you have found out. *What might have happened to it in its journey to you?*

Perform the poem

Re-read the poem, and think about how you can emphasise the drama of the poem in your performance. Think about how you could use your voice to create the rise and fall in the journey – where will you speed up, where will you slow down, where you will make your voice louder or quieter, where you might take a pause, where lines need to run into each other. Practice a few times to perfect this. Consider how to use your facial expressions and body movements to add to the storytelling, making sure these add to, but don't detract from the meaning of the words and the emotions evoked by the poem. Perform this to a friend or family member and ask for their reactions.

Activate your imagination

Think about an element in nature that interests you. It could be a seed, plant or flower, a particular creature, or a physical feature like a river. Take a piece of paper and a pen and write down why this element of nature interests you. In the same way that you researched rock formation, find out more about your chosen element of nature. Bring your ideas together by considering what you might want to tell someone else about this element of nature and why it is special. *How will you make them see how special this thing is? How will you show you understand them, how they came into being, how they behave, what they do and why they are important?* When you have some ideas written down, see if you can use these to make your own poem about the element of nature you have chosen. You could also have a go at illustrating your poem, like Junli Song has done for *Don't Be Bored Rock*.

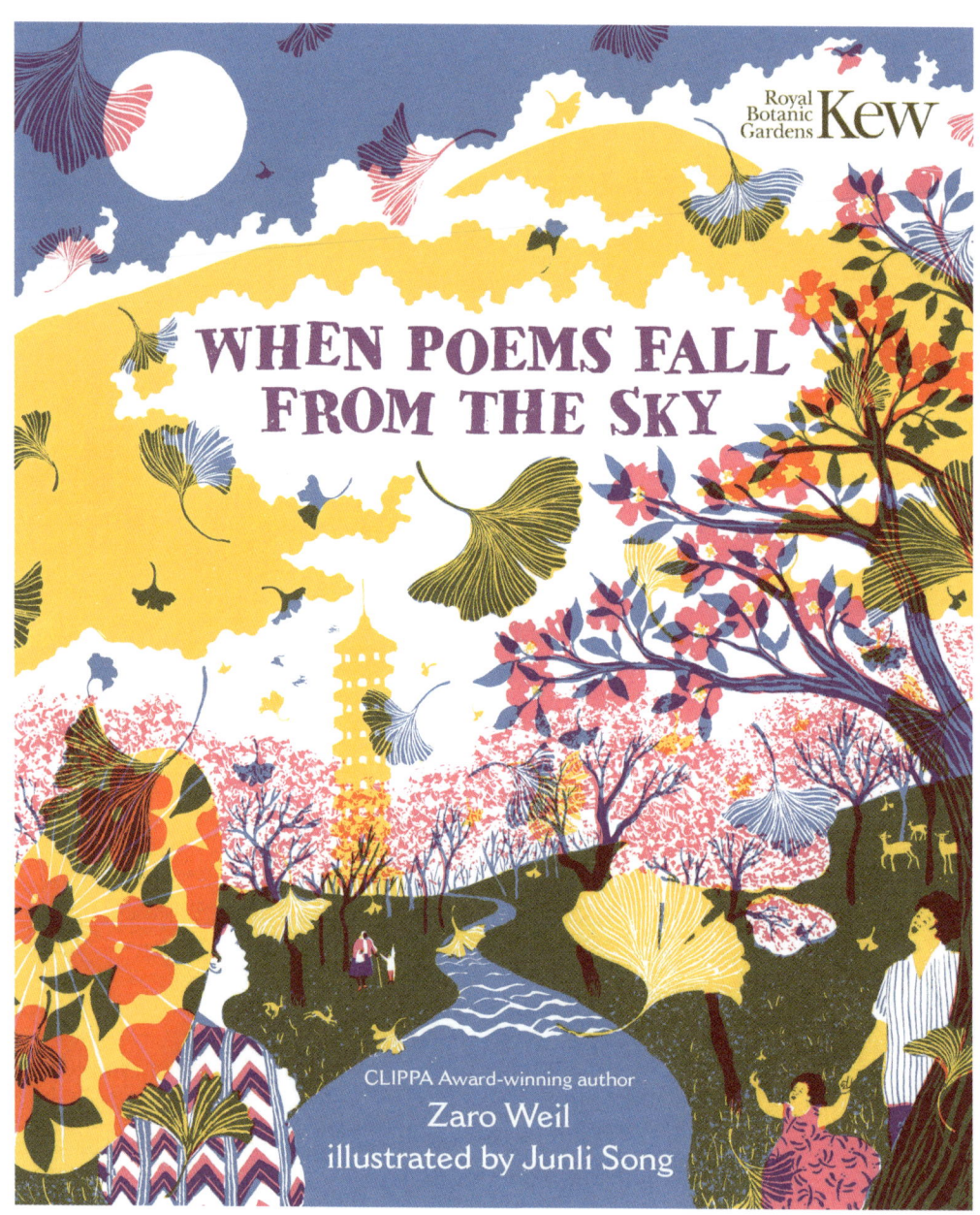

Also available from Zaro Weil and Junli Song

WHEN POEMS FALL FROM THE SKY

In association with the Royal Botanic Gardens, Kew

In this exquisite, fantastical and eye-popping anthology, published in association with The Royal Botanic Gardens, Kew, Mother Nature shares dazzling poems, hilarious rhymes and heart-warming little plays with us. From rapping fungi and magical seeds to flying wizards and ten quintillion parading bugs, every page bursts with the colour, mystery and sheer delight of the natural world, and is a must-have for every bookshelf.

WHEN POEMS FALL FROM THE SKY is a book to be shared with the whole family, a tender love letter to Earth, reminding each of us that we are all guardians of our planet.

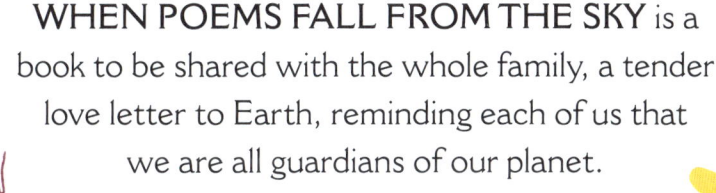

ABOUT THE AUTHOR AND ILLUSTRATOR

Zaro Weil lives on a little farm in southern France. She loves writing and animals and trees and making things up. She has had a lot of fun working with Junli on her fourth children's book, *Cherry Moon*.

(Other Books By Zaro: *Mud, Moon and Me*, *Firecrackers*, *Spot Guevara Hero Dog*, *Polka Dot Poems* and *When Poems fall from the Sky*)

(Zaro's website: zaroweil.com)

Junli Song lives in Chicago in America. She loves colours and patterns and telling stories and printmaking. She has had a wonderful time working on her first book *Cherry Moon* with Zaro.

(Junli's website: www.artsofsong.com)